Manifestation of
the Sons of God

McClinton E. Porter

PRESS

DEDICATION

First and foremost I dedicate this book to the triune God; Father, Son, and Holy Spirit. I am overwhelmed that the Lord would choose to use me to produce this work. For Your glory, and Your glory alone Lord.

To my wife Tammie, I am so appreciative of the way you have supported me over the past twenty years. I love you more than words can express. You are truly my good thing.

To my children Bernita, Bryce, Kiersten, and Jeremiah, each of you continue to be a source of inspiration for me.

To my father McClinton Porter Jr., Thank you for being an excellent example of what a father should be.

ACKNOWLEDGEMENTS

*P*astor Emeritus Obadiah and Sarah LaFlora who taught me how to walk with the Lord.

Pastors Stephen and Candy LaFlora who are true Holy Ghost friends and have helped facilitate my spiritual development.

The Maranatha Church family who has prayed for me and my family and loved us unconditionally.

Pastor Reuben S. Robinson who walked with me in the beginning and is a true friend in every sense of the word.

Rev. Dr. Forrest James Robinson for your invaluable encouragement.

All the pastors and ministers of the gospel who have mentored me from afar via your writing and media ministries.

All of my brothers and sisters in the body of Christ who have helped me arrive at this place.

.

ENDORSEMENTS

"Manifestation of the Sons of God" is an excellent portrayal of the clarion call issued by our Father God to all of His children to rise up and take their place in the kingdom of God. For too long, God's people have lived beneath the privileges afforded them per their spiritual birthright. McClinton Porter issues a challenge to all believers to make a commitment to learn of God's original design for humanity to mature in their knowledge of "kingdom sonship." The revelation of sonship unveiled in this book is vital for the end-time revival, as the whole creation awaits the relief that will be provided when the sons of God assume their God-given role. Read it and be blessed. Learn, rise up, and take your place as a "son of God!"

Pastor Stephen LaFlora, M.S. – Senior Pastor Maranatha Church, Chicago, IL.

If you are one of those Christians who has the idea that you are "just an old sinner saved by grace," then read this book. The author helps us to understand that being a new creation in Christ brings with it an indelible imprint of God's glory upon us. I believe that the author in these writings shows us that with this glory comes an assignment that demands our demonstration of what manifest sons of God look and act like in the earth realm. Open yourself up to receive this revelation.

Rev. Obadiah LaFlora, M.Ed., M.A.T.S. – Founder and Pastor Emeritus – Maranatha Church, Chicago, IL.

This book has provoked me to aspire to walk in the fullness of sonship. As a result, I am more convinced now than ever before that as I continue to allow the Holy Spirit to transform me I will certainly see His glory revealed in a greater measure. The author does an extraordinary job of teaching how to live as a son of God. I encourage you to add this to the top of your must read list.

Tammie Porter, M.Ed. – Director of Children's Ministry Maranatha Church, Chicago, IL.

This is a life-changing work full of thought provoking revelation. It issues a challenge to us all to grow in our faith and develop a closer, more intimate walk with the Lord. This book fills a great need to help us become true sons of God. It is a valuable resource for anyone that has determined to live for God's glory and His glory alone.

Reuben S. Robinson - Pastor Life Changing Ministries International

Many times, prior to the word of God being preached, you will hear the minister pray, "Lord let your word come forth with great clarity, for we desire to be transformed as we embrace your truths!" In "Manifestation of the Sons of God" this prayer is answered. It was exciting for me to experience my spirit stretching to receive the truth presented in this Spirit-filled work! This book contains fruit producing revelation, wisdom, and knowledge. God breathed on this one!

Rev. Dr. Forrest James Robinson

Table of Contents

❦

Introduction

*F*ebruary 2, 1992 was the most momentous occasion in my life. Now don't get me wrong, I have had many noteworthy experiences. The day I got married and the birth of my children are among those that I consider life-changing. But none compare to February 2, 1992, for this was the day I said yes once and for all to the living God. Yes, this was the day I was born into the family of God. I mention this because though I had no real knowledge of God (I was a heathen in every sense of the word), once I was born-again by the Spirit of God almost instantaneously I began to have a sense of the responsibility that accompanies being a child of God. This sense of responsibility set me on a quest that has produced this book as its fruit.

I vividly recall soon after giving my life to the Lord being hit with an onslaught by the forces of darkness which resulted in my yielding to sin. I am so thankful that there were godly people in my life to help restore me. This incident made it clear to me that we are definitely in a battle, and if I were going to win I had better learn to fight, and how to fight properly. So I prayed and asked God what I needed to do to walk this walk, and live a life that would bring glory and honor to Him. Immediately I heard that still, small voice say to me...son, stay in My word and continually seek Me in prayer.

As I endeavored to comply with the Lord's instruction to me, a marvelous thing began to happen. I began to realize that being a Christian meant far more than going to weekly Bible study and attending church on Sunday, though these are certainly things that committed Christians should do. The Holy Spirit of the living God began to help me see that as those who profess the name of Christ, we owe it to God, as members of His family, to be for a lost, dying, sin-sick humanity everything He created us to be!

Armed with this revelation, through the years I have studied the Bible to try to not only grasp what this entailed, but to make it a lifestyle. Romans 8:19-21 (Amplified Bible) *says "For [even the whole] creation (all nature) waits and longs earnestly for God's sons to be made known [waits for the revealing, the disclosing of their sonship]. For the creation (nature) was subjected to frailty (to futility, condemned to frustration), not because of some intentional fault on its part, but by the will of Him Who subjected it-[yet] with the hope that nature (creation) itself will be set free from its bondage to decay and corruption [and gain an entrance] into the glorious freedom of God's children."* Wow! What a tremendous privilege and responsibility we have as sons (children) of God.

The purpose of this book is to help you realize what it means to be a son of God, who you are as a son of God, and how to live life in this earth realm as a son of God. I certainly don't regard myself as the foremost authority on this subject, but I am thankful for what the Holy Spirit has shown me relative to this. I believe that as you endeavor to internalize the truths of God's word delineated in this book your walk with the Lord will be revolutionized.

My earnest prayer is that as you read this book, the eyes of your heart will be flooded with light, that new revelation will be added to what you already have, and you will be manifest to the world in ever-increasing measure as a son of God.

Rev. McClinton Elliott Porter

Foreword

𝓶 y vocation as a physician has had many effects on my personal development as a son of God. There are some skills that I have acquired and over time they have been greatly developed with the many experiences that I have encountered. Then there are the gifts I received from God Himself as He uniquely fashioned me from conception (predestined Romans 8:29, 30) for His glory and His purpose. With that being said, if I were to summarize my usual mode of approach, I would have to say that I look things up and I pay close attention to detail. First I observe, then I dissect, and finally I determine. The term "discern" comes to the mind as I try to illustrate my typical "modus operandi."

When I looked up the definition of manifestation, of all the many choices available, the one that caught my full attention was the one that read, "An indication that something is present, real, or exists." This next statement is a little out of context regarding the core or the essence of this book, but it works out because I do not wish to prematurely divulge any of the great contents of this succinct masterpiece (don't want to spoil it for you) but I have to say it. God is present in this work! Yes HE is!

It is obvious that my dear friend and author of this great effort, Rev. McClinton Elliott Porter, was accompanied and led by the Holy Spirit as he penned these relevant statements, questions, and reflections, all confirmed by the Word of God. The lines are full, even rich, with revelation. Both the saved and "not yet saved" individual will be moved to a place of change and/or decision. Rev. Porter serves us all as a teacher, preacher, and historian, and comes across exactly as the virtuous man that he is.

Every once in a while we are fortunate enough to detect the true excitement occurring in our spirit being. I felt my inner man delighting in the Word of God (Romans 7:22). I desired more! I pray that the reader is equally, if not even more blessed and edified by this impactful read. I think the author will not have a problem as I too extend the invitation to you all to experience the manifestation of your God given sonship!

Rev. Dr. Forrest James Robinson

Chapter 1

Glory from the Beginning

God said, Let Us [Father, Son, and Holy Spirit] make man-kind in Our image, after Our likeness, and let them have complete authority over the fish of the sea, the birds of the air, and over everything that creeps upon the earth. So God created man in His own image, in the image and likeness of God He created him; male and female He created them. And God blessed them and said to them, Be fruitful, multiply, and fill the earth, and subdue it [using all its vast resources in the service of God and man]; and have dominion over the fish of the sea, the birds of the air, and over every living crea-ture that moves upon the earth (Genesis 1:26-28 Amplified Bible.)

7 often think of what it must have been like for the man and the woman in the Garden of Eden during their time of perfection; when sin was as alien to them as an alien would be to us today. I try to envision in my mind's eye how those walks and talks with God "in the cool of the day" affected them (Genesis 3:8 KJV). I think about how refreshing they must have been, how intimate, how awe-inspiring, how glorious.

I've wondered whether Adam received a download of wisdom and knowledge and instantaneously knew things, or if God had to teach Him how to utilize what He put in him. Whatever the case, I believe I am on solid ground when I say it surely must have been heaven on earth. Well beloved, God is the same yesterday, today, and forever (Malachi 3:6; Hebrews 13:8 KJV). If it was heaven on earth for them I am convinced that we should confidently be able to make the same declaration and share the same experience in the here and now!

Many wonderful sermons have been preached, and many wonderful books have been written that place special emphasis on realizing our purpose for existing. In the inner-most recesses of every human being dwells the innate desire to know and realize that there is something special about them— that they are here to allow greatness to manifest in them and through them. Little children start out daring to believe the impossible. As soon as they are able, they begin communicating grandiose dreams to anyone who will listen, readily displaying a God-given desire and ability to dream, and dream big. Well, all we have to do is understand purpose to know why this is the case; but to understand purpose we have to know the original intent of the Creator who ascribed purpose to each and every life.

Language is the medium through which human beings communicate. Communication occurs only when a message is transmitted, received, and understood. If all three don't occur then communication hasn't transpired. Communication provides the parameters within which we, as social creatures, establish shared meaning. I should note here that once a communication is understood it typically elicits a response. Responding is an act of the will and a lack of response doesn't necessarily indicate that communication hasn't occurred.

God's Plan

God used some extraordinary language in communicating His description of and purpose for humanity. First, He said we are made in His image and after His likeness (Genesis 1:26). Hearing those words immediately creates in our minds an impression of the magnitude of their meaning. The word image refers to something in the sense of a replica; but even more significant is the fact that it refers to the essential nature of something. Similarly, the word likeness refers to the original after which a thing is patterned. So what God is endeavoring to communicate is that He created a being called man (humanity), who is a replica of God, possessing His essential nature, and patterned after the original, which is God Himself. Wow! How awesome! This is the message that God has transmitted. This is His plan not only from the beginning of time, but from eternity. But until we (the recipients of the intended communication) receive, understand, & respond appropriately to it, we won't realize the potential of it in our lives.

Romans 12:1-2 (Amplified Bible) states *"I Appeal to you therefore, brethren, and beg of you in view of [all] the mercies of God, to make a decisive dedication of your bodies [presenting all your members and faculties] as a living sacrifice, holy (devoted, consecrated) and well pleasing to God, which is your reasonable (rational, intelligent) service and spiritual worship. Do not be conformed to this world (this age), [fashioned after and adapted to its external, superficial customs], but be transformed (changed) by the [entire] renewal of your mind [by its new ideals and its new attitude], so that you may prove [for yourselves] what is the good and acceptable and perfect will of God, even the thing which is good and acceptable and perfect [in His sight for you].* I feel it is necessary that I interject here how crucial it is to internalize these verses of Scripture, for without doing so you will have difficulty putting into practice everything else I will be discussing in this book. There are three indispensable keys here that I want to point out before moving forward.

First, it is imperative that we present our entire being to God. This is an all at once occurrence that manifests itself through the process of continual obedience. In other words, once we decide with finality this is the course of action we will take, we then have to walk it out through obedience to the word of God. Secondly, we can't do things the way the world does, i.e., fashioned after and adapted to its external, superficial customs. The Bible still says whoever wants to be a friend of the world makes themselves an enemy of God (James 4:4). Lastly, but certainly not of least importance, we must be transformed. The Greek word translated transformed is *metamorphoo* (pronounced met·am·or·**fo**·o) which means a change into another form, to change the essential nature, literally to be changed into an entirely different species of being[1]. This word paints the picture of a caterpillar going into a cocoon and emerging as a beautiful butterfly, an entirely different species. In order for this transformation to occur we have to begin to think like God thinks and that will only happen if we give His word and His Spirit a position of preeminence in our lives.

Created for Glory

What an awesome plan God has for mankind. His plan for us is glory from the beginning and glory for all eternity. In fact, in her book *The Blood and the Glory,* Billye Brim describes the Bible as "The story of the glory."[2] Typically, when we begin to think about the glory, we conceive of it as something that is abstract and ethereal, that is to say, "Otherworldly." And though it is Otherworldly in that it

emanates from God, God's plan is that we not limit our-
selves to experiencing it in this realm (earth) in a random
manner, but that we habitually abide in His glory. Therefore,
it is imperative that we have a clear understanding of what
glory is.

The glory of God refers to His perfections, His attributes
and characteristics. Glory also refers to the manifestation
of God's presence in this natural realm, in a tangible way,
often accompanied by physical phenomena. Hence the primary Hebrew word for glory in the Old Testament is kabowd
(pronounced kaw-**bode**) which means weight or heaviness,
conveying worthiness. That is why many times when God's
glory is manifested it is difficult to remain standing because
of the weight or heaviness of His presence. This is also
referred to as the "Shekinah." This is seen in 1 Kings 8:10-
11: *"When the priests had come out of the Holy Place, the
cloud filled the Lord's house. So the priests could not stand
to minister because of the cloud, for the glory of the Lord
had filled the Lord's house"* (Amplified Bible). It also refers
to splendor, majesty, the manifestation of power, and the
attribution of high status[3].

King David, the "sweet psalmist of Israel," got a revelation of this when he stated with obvious awe and wonder in

Psalm 8 vv. 4-6 *"What is man that You are mindful of him, and the son of [earthborn] man that You care for him? Yet You have made him but a little lower than God [or heavenly beings] and You have crowned him with glory and honor. You made him to have dominion over the works of Your hands; You have put all things under his feet"* (Amplified Bible). Wow! This scripture declares that God created man (human beings) just a little lower than Himself. Now, many English translations of the Bible say that man was created a little lower than the angels, but the actual Hebrew word used in this passage (that some translate as angels) is *Elohim* (pronounced el-o-**heem**) which is used to denote the triune God; Father, Son, and Holy Spirit. It is the same word used for God in Genesis 1:1 and 1:26.

After ascribing to man such a lofty position God endowed him with what he would need to fulfill his role and responsibilities. He crowned (literally enveloped or completely surrounded) man with glory and honor. In other words, God Himself qualified man to be His partner in ruling by placing in and upon him His very own attributes and characteristics and giving him dominion, that is to say, complete and total control and authority over His creation up to the throne of God. He ascribed to angels the responsibility of serving

(Hebrews 1:14) but to Adam (mankind) he ascribed the responsibility of ruling and the high status that accompanies it. Hallelujah!

Chaper 2

Adam, Where art Thou?
꒳

And the Lord God took the man and put him in the Garden of Eden to tend and guard and keep it. And the Lord God commanded the man, saying, You may freely eat of every tree of the garden; But of the tree of the knowledge of good and evil and blessing and calamity you shall not eat, for in the day that you eat of it you shall surely die (Genesis 2:15-17 Amplified Bible)......But the Lord God called to Adam and said to him, Where are you? (Genesis 3:9 Amplified Bible)

Created to Rule

*G*od bestowed upon Adam (mankind) a tremendous privilege, the privilege of ruling and reigning with God and on His behalf in the earth realm (Psalm 115:16

KJV). Why God chose earth, or why He chose man, I don't know; I imagine eternity will reveal it. But I must say, as one who has his human origin in Adam, I'm certainly glad that God chose mankind to rule as opposed to bestowing this honor on some other facet of His creation.

God placed Adam, the representative man, in the Garden of Eden. This was the place where God desired man to be, the place where man could fulfill his destiny. Eden is referred to as paradise and it literally means a place or state of bliss, happiness, and delight, i.e., a place of extraordinary pleasure. How awesome it is that we serve a God who places us in an environment overflowing with extraordinary pleasure and delight in order for us to fulfill the eternal plan and purpose He has declared for us. I am of the opinion; in fact I am convinced that the greatest degree of pleasure we will ever realize is the result of being in the center of God's will, experiencing His presence and His glory in an intimate way. Psalm 16:11 declares *"You will show me the path of life; in Your presence is fullness of joy, at your right hand there are pleasures forevermore" (Amplified Bible).* This isn't something we have to wait until the great by and by to experience, we can have it right here and right now; provided we meet God's conditions.

Adam was instructed to do two things in the garden, tend it and guard it. After making sure that man had abundant provision, the very next thing God bestowed upon him was stewardship, which is defined as the careful and responsible management of something entrusted to one's care. In tending the garden Adam was to cultivate it and foster its growth. In other words Adam was to use the giftedness he received from his Creator to cause his environment to fulfill its God-given purpose, which is to ultimately glorify God.

You might say, well how can a garden glorify God? My answer to that is the same way that the heavens can. Psalm 19:1(Amplified Bible) says *"THE HEAVENS declare the glory of God; and the firmament shows and proclaims His handiwork."* Simply put, the vastness of the heavens testifies to the immensity of God; their awe-inspiring splendor declares the glory and perfections of the Creator, the God of the universe, the living God. Consequently, the heavens fulfill their God-given purpose. By revealing His glory the heavens glorify God.

The earth received from God everything it needed to fulfill its purpose; which was to produce on behalf of mankind as they fulfilled the mandate to be fruitful, multiply, replenish (literally fill) the earth, and subdue it, i.e., subjugate it or make it obey (Genesis 1:28). Yes beloved, the earth was programmed to glorify God by responding to mankind's authority in it and over it. We will discuss this mind-boggling level of authority that Adam (as the representative of humanity) had in more detail later, particularly in chapters six and seven. Suffice it to say, this is certainly a reality (truth based on what Scripture proclaims) of which we as believers need to receive ever-increasing revelation.

Now, I know that religion has taught us many things, and in the time that I've been walking with the Lord I've come to discover that many things that religious tradition teaches doesn't line up with what God has proclaimed! In fact Jesus went so far as to say that the religious traditions that the people of His day clung to made God's word ineffective (Mark 7:13). I personally believe this happens because people equate their personal experience with the totality of what God's word will produce. For example, when someone's experience doesn't include health and healing there is a propensity for them to say that God doesn't heal anymore. If someone refuses to obey God's word regarding the tithe and free-will offerings through which we cause the law of sowing and reaping (Galatians 6:7; Genesis 8:22, 1Corinthians 9:6) to work in our favor, and they continue to experience lack and insufficiency, there is a propensity among them to boldly proclaim that Jesus said "the poor will be with you always," as if poverty and lack is a badge of honor. Beloved, if our experience isn't lining up with God's word then know of a surety that the problem isn't with the word of God. Today we have an abundance of information made readily available to us, but what is desperately needed is revelation of the reality that every word of God works when the hearer of the word mixes it with faith (Hebrews 4:2-3)!

By now I'm sure you may be wondering why I am mentioning this. Well, the answer to that is, if you are unable to accept what God's word says by faith, instead of trying to explain it away, the rest of this book won't benefit you. As we proceed it is imperative that we understand certain Scriptural truths. As I expound upon them, they may be review for some of you and for others it may be the first time you've heard anything like this. Whatever the case, I believe that you will be able to glean some benefit as you continue reading.

The god-man

In order to embrace and fully realize your purpose and destiny it is essential to understand God's original plan and purpose. Unfortunately, I have found that far too frequently many of those who have received Jesus minimize what the Old Testament has to say. This is a grave error and I hope that you who are reading this book don't fall into that category. I think that the terms Old Testament and New Testament lead to this way of thinking. Actually, it may be more practical, in order to help understand the significance of the totality of Scripture, to refer to them as the first covenant and second covenant. Jesus said that He **"came to fulfill the law and the prophets"** (Matthew 5:17). The Holy Spirit reminds us through the Apostle Paul that **"all Scripture is given by inspiration of God"** (2 Timothy 3:16).

Scripture refers to Adam as the son of God (Luke 3:38). Now I certainly am not a geneticist, but I have learned a couple of things about genetic constitution. In order to qualify as someone's son you must contain their deoxyribonucleic acid (DNA). In possessing someone's DNA you become hard-wired with their essential nature and characteristics. In fact, medical science has determined that every human being is essentially the same genetically, with less than 1 percent of genes (called alleles) being different between people. This difference is what accounts for the distinction in physical appearance[4]. So for Adam to be called the son of God, of necessity he possessed God's essential nature and characteristics. The entire human race was in Adam because from one blood comes every nation (ethnicity) of man (Acts 17:26). Pause for a moment and think about the reality and the magnitude of that statement.

Adam was of God and from the earth, that is to say he simultaneously possessed natural characteristics (that which is from the earth) and divine characteristics which he received when God breathed into him the breath of life (Genesis 2:7). Hence, God's plan was for Adam to rule in the natural realm and the spirit realm just as God does. Hallelujah! It's important to understand that God is sovereign and that all things are from Him, for Him, and to Him; but it is equally important to understand that He gave Adam (mankind) dominion, that is to say complete and total control and authority, over God's creation. This was and is God's plan! Adam was the god-man, made in the image and likeness of God, destined to exercise kingly dominion like God, subject only to the authority of God.

Now I know some of you may be referring to me as a blasphemer because I referred to Adam as the god-man. But as the representative or prototype for mankind that's exactly what he was. I heard Pastor Rod Parsley once say (and I paraphrase) "it's amazing that we freely refer to people as a man or woman of God and don't think twice about it, but the moment we refer to someone as a god-man people get in an uproar." But this is exactly how Scripture refers to Adam. It simply means that Adam had a divine nature that emanates from God and an earthly nature from which his humanity is derived. Hence, he was the god-man. Because we were in Adam from the beginning, this is how God would refer to everyone that came from Adam once they entered the earth realm by being born of a woman (see Psalm 82:6 & John 10:31-39). What an awesome plan by an awesome, holy, and majestic God. HALLELUJAH!

Treason

God required Adam to fulfill one condition. He required the strictest obedience. As long as Adam (mankind) obeyed God they would rule and reign with God in unbroken fellowship. It would literally be, as I previously mentioned, heaven on earth continually. I am pretty confident that you are familiar with the account of the fall of man that occurred in the Garden of Eden, but I ask that you indulge me as I point out several things regarding this incident.

First of all, God placed the man (male, i.e. Adam) in the garden and instructed him to tend and guard and keep it (Genesis 2:15 Amplified Bible). That means Adam was to watch over the garden and make sure that it fulfilled its God-given purpose. In other words, he was to use his authority to oppose and overcome anything that contradicted the instructions he received from God. Immediately after this we see God giving Adam free reign over everything except for one tree, the tree of the knowledge of good and evil (Genesis 2:16-17). God told him not to eat of it. This tree was separated unto God, thus it was holy. I'm sure many of you can recall being told by your parents not to touch certain things because they belonged to them, and also being informed of the dire consequences you would encounter for disobedience. The thing to remember here is that God has reserved certain things for Himself and because we love, respect, and honor Him, we should refrain from violating His instructions regarding them.

It's important to note that the woman was still in Adam at this point. She was yet to be physically manifest in the earth realm. God determined that Adam needed one suitable (properly equipped) to help him, a bride as it were. This is symbolic of the relationship between Christ and the Church. She was taken out of Adam and he declared of her *"this is bone of my bones and flesh of my flesh."* The text goes on to state *"Therefore shall a man leave his father and his mother, and shall cleave unto his wife: and they shall be one flesh"* (Genesis 2:23-24). Just as Christ, as the Head, and His body (the church) is one, Adam, that is to say, mankind (male and female) were created to be unified in a covenant (marriage) relationship (see Ephesians 5:21-33). Once the woman was manifest in the earth the man, Adam, was to instruct her as to what God required, and together they were to subdue the earth (use all of its vast resources in the service of God and man). This is significant because the only way to exercise God-given authority is to be in unity. In the absence of unity there is strife, and where there is strife there is confusion and every evil work (James 3:14-16).

So everything was lovely in paradise. The man and the woman were enjoying God and being enjoyed by Him, enjoying one another, and enjoying ruling and reigning as regents in this realm. Consequently, their faith was tested. We must, as believers, be constantly aware that our faith is going to be tested. In fact, the Apostle James stated for the believer to *"Consider it wholly joyful, my brethren, whenever you are enveloped in or encounter trials of any sort or fall into various temptations. Be assured and understand that the trial and proving of your faith bring out endurance and steadfastness and patience"* (James 1:2-3 Amplified Bible). Scripture records that the serpent, Satan, entered the garden and began to talk to the woman. This was the faith test.

I find it interesting that the tempter approached the woman instead of the man, Adam. I believe this was very strategic on his part, as it can be inferred from the Scriptural context regarding the fall (Genesis 3) that the woman learned what God said from Adam, not directly from God as Adam had. According to 1 Timothy 2:14 (Amplified Bible), *"and it was not Adam who was deceived, but [the] woman who was deceived and deluded and fell into transgression."* Experience has taught me that it is a lot easier to be deceived when you receive information second-hand as opposed to receiving it directly from the source. This Scripture verse informs us that the woman "fell" into transgression because she was deceived and deluded. The Greek word for deceive is apatao (pronounced ap-at-**ah**-o) and literally means to delude, which implies deceiving so thoroughly as to obscure the truth; and beguile, which stresses the use of charm and persuasion in the act of deceiving. Because people don't typically fall intentionally, the woman fell into transgression as the result of being enticed to believe and act on twisted truth, not because she was seeking to rebel against God.

Adam, on the other hand committed high treason, which is defined as the betrayal of trust, and the offense of attempting by overt acts to overthrow the government to which the offender owes allegiance. Adam knew full well what he was doing. He heard and understood God's command clearly. He knew the consequences for disobedience. Yet, he chose his own will, disregarded the priceless stewardship with which he had been entrusted, and handed over the authority to exercise dominion in this realm to a rogue, rebellious, renegade spirit...Satan! In an instant he descended from the highest position among God's creation to the low estate of being subservient to one whose ultimate goal was to destroy God's intimate friend. I imagine that's why it's referred to as the fall, and what a horrific fall it was.

As God showed up for His usual walk and talk with Adam, a strange thing happened; Adam neglected to attend

(Genesis 3:8-9). God called out to Adam and asked him "Where art thou?" Now certainly God knew where He was, but He wanted Adam to locate himself. It was evident Adam and the woman (she wasn't called Eve yet) knew something had changed between them and God because they tried to hide from Him. Sin (placing our own will over the known will of God) causes disharmony between God and man and will always cause man to try to hide and make excuses, rather than own up to it and receive God's mercy. Adam had to face the reality that he was now separated from God, and I'm sure that was a terrifying proposition for him. One transgression, just one, turned their world upside down. They knew the verdict was guilty as charged. I wonder what must have been going through their minds as they waited for the Judge of the entire universe to pronounce their sentence. I imagine Adam hung his head in shame and was tormented by the thought of what his rebellion would produce. It seemed as if Satan had won. As bad as it was, this incident didn't catch God by surprise. God had the end figured out before there was a beginning, and in judgment, mercy would be revealed that would produce eternal hope! Hallelujah!

Chapter 3

The Promise that Produces Hope

And the man said, The woman whom You gave to be with me – she gave me [fruit] from the tree, and I ate. And the Lord God said to the woman, What is this you have done? And the woman said, the serpent beguiled (cheated, outwitted, and deceived) me, and I ate….And I will put enmity between you and the woman, and between your offspring and her Offspring; He will bruise and tread your head underfoot, and you will lie in wait and bruise His heel (Genesis 3:12-13, 15 Amplified Bible).

There they were, standing before the God of the universe, guilty of rebellion and treason. I am reminded of the times during my childhood and adolescence where I stood in my father's presence after having violated his instructions to me. I remember the feelings of guilt, shame, and fear that overwhelmed me. I remember being too ashamed and too afraid to look in his face, while simultaneously hoping that I could catch his eye with a look that would elicit his mercy and not his judgment. I realize now that even though at times I received judgment, that his judgment was replete with mercy.

In an instant the man and the woman had experienced spiritual death. God's instruction had been violated and there were consequences to be doled out. As I mentioned in the preceding chapter, God told Adam that if he violated His instruction he would surely die. What was so horrific about the present circumstance was that God never intended for Adam (mankind) to experience death. Death simply means separation from the source of life. We know that God is the source of life and that He is spirit (John 4:24). Therefore the initial death that Adam experienced was spiritual, which would ultimately produce physical death. What we have to understand is that after sin entered in, if their spiritual union with God remained intact, Adam (the male and female) would have been annihilated, completely obliterated, and mankind would have ceased to exist. God is so holy that sin can't dwell in His presence. It (sin) would instantaneously be consumed by his glory and holiness. God is light and in Him is no darkness. So even in judgment we can see the ubiquitous presence of God's mercy.

Additionally, God had given His word that man (humanity) would have dominion over all of God's creation. If man ceased to exist then God's word would have been proven to be false, reducing Him to the status of liar. If God had been proven to be a liar I imagine He couldn't be God anymore. But hallelujah, God had a plan from eternity. He already knew how He would restore mankind to oneness with Himself and this time no outside force would ever separate man from God again. The only thing that could and would keep mankind separated from God would be the exercise of his own will to reject God and choose his own way instead of God's way.

As all the guilty parties stood before Him, the serpent, the man, and the woman; God began to mete out the judgment that resulted from their rebellion. Beginning with the serpent, the snake who was the embodiment of the devil, He decreed their respective consequences. Throughout Scripture Satan is referred to as the serpent (Revelation 12:9, 20:2; 2 Corinthians 11:3). The snake has come to represent all that is revolting, repulsive, and low. The Bible describes the serpent as being more subtle, that is to say more cunning, crafty, devious, and shrewd than all the beasts of the field (Genesis 3:1). How fitting that Satan would use the body of such a creature, one whose characteristics were strikingly similar to his own, to gain entrance into the physical earth realm in order to interact with those who governed this realm.

God began to speak, and as Adam and the woman waited with baited breath, they heard these words spoken to the serpent; "...*You are cursed above all [domestic] animals and above every [wild] living thing of the field*" (Genesis 3:14 Amplified Bible). If this was the penalty the snake incurred for being a facilitator, I imagine Adam believed that their punishment would be far worse for actually transgressing the commandment of God. The feeling of isolation and loneliness must have been devastating. They waited. Instead of their hearts being full of the spiritual force of faith it was now consumed with a spiritual force that had previously been foreign to them, the force of fear. How unfathomable the darkness and despair of that moment must have been. They waited. It must have seemed like an eternity. They waited.

Then God began to speak to the spiritual snake, that renegade spirit Satan. Judgment was pronounced. God said to Satan *"And I will put enmity between you and the woman, and between your offspring and her Offspring; He will bruise and tread your head underfoot, and you will lie in wait and bruise his heel"* (Genesis 3:15 Amplified Bible). Satan's relationship with God had been eternally severed when he led the rebellion in heaven (see Isaiah 14, Ezekiel 28, and Revelation 12); now his relationship with man, who is God's premier creation, was being established for eternity. The relationship would be one that was founded upon enmity. Now that word doesn't sound like anything good. The Hebrew word for enmity is ebah (pronounced ay-**baw**) and means hatred and animosity between two parties or even classes of beings.[5] When Adam heard these words I'm sure his eyes lit up. I'm sure he felt like he was dreaming to hear such good news.

Well you may be thinking how can having an eternal enemy be good news? It wasn't having an enemy that Adam viewed as good news, it was the fact that there would be a seed (Offspring), emanating from the woman, that would ultimately destroy their enemy once and for all. The reality of this truth assured Adam and the woman that God wasn't discarding them like yesterday's trash. Even though Adam had committed the ultimate transgression, God, in His mercy and faithfulness to His word, provided hope for mankind while simultaneously demonstrating His wisdom.

It's important to note the language God used. He declared that the seed of the woman would destroy the enemy. Well that's fine and good except for one small detail; women don't produce seed men do. Women receive seed, and once germination occurs, the produce of that germination (new life) grows and develops in the earth (womb), and at the appropriate time the harvest (a new human being) comes forth (see Mark 4:26-29). Of course the promised seed being referred to is Jesus. God couldn't use Adam's seed because his nature was now sinful and corrupt, as would be that of every human being born after the fall. If Jesus had come from the seed of a man he would have inherited Adam's sinful nature and needed a savior Himself. God determined He would bypass the normal natural process and remind the entire human family that He is a supernatural God and as His offspring we were born to operate in this same supernatural power and ability. HALLELUJAH!

Fast forward with me about 4000 years after this scene in the Garden of Eden to the city of Nazareth in Palestine, as a young lady, engaged to a carpenter, has a supernatural encounter. The encounter is reported as follows: *And the angel said to her, "Do not be afraid Mary, for you have found grace (free, spontaneous, absolute favor and loving-kindness) with God. And listen! You will become pregnant and will give birth to a Son, and you shall call His name Jesus." And Mary said to the angel, "How can this be, since I have no [intimacy with any man as a] husband?" Then the angel said to her, "The Holy Spirit will come upon you, and the power of the Most High will overshadow you [like a shining cloud]; and so the holy (pure, sinless) Thing (Offspring) shall be born of you will be called the Son of God...For with God nothing is ever impossible and no word from God shall be without power or impossible of fulfillment"* (Luke 1: 30-31, 34-35, 37 Amplified Bible).

God took what the woman had to give (her egg cell) as a seed and by His Spirit infused it with His very own life. Hence the seed of the woman, Jesus the God-man, the last Adam, was manifest in this realm and it was the result of the promise that God gave in Genesis 3:15. It was indeed the promise that produced hope!

Chapter 4

We Need a Blood Transfusion

The blood shall be for a token or sign to you [upon the doorposts of] the houses where you are, [that] when I see the blood, I will pass over you, and no plague shall be upon you to destroy you when I smite the land of Egypt (Exodus 12:13 Amplified Bible)...For the life of the body is in its blood. I have given you the blood upon the altar to purify you, making you right with the Lord. It is the blood, given in exchange for a life, that makes purification possible (Leviticus 17:11 NLT)...After supper he took another cup of wine and said "This cup is the new covenant between God and his people – an agreement confirmed with my blood, which is poured out as a sacrifice for you (Luke 22:20 NLT).

*I*f you recall, in Chapter 1 I stated that mankind was created for glory. Prior to Adam's transgression, The Scripture says *"And they were both naked, the man and his wife, and were not ashamed"* (Genesis 2:25). After the fall we see them hiding because they realized that they were naked (Genesis 3:10). Now it's true that they didn't have on any clothes because it goes on to say that God made coats of skins and clothed them (Genesis 3:21). My question is why was it an issue now when previously it wasn't even a consideration? The answer beloved is that previously they were clothed with the glory of God, and the glory adds beauty and holiness to everything it abides in and/or on. The glory of God contains everything that God is. In fact there had been so much glory on them that it took Adam over 900 years after the fall to learn how to die!

The Mystery of Blood

There was a key component in Adam's constitution that made it possible for mankind to be infused with the glory of God, and that component was (and still is) blood. In spite of the reality that mankind has discovered a wealth of knowledge regarding blood and its value, blood still remains a mystery. The reason for this is that blood contains both natural and spiritual life, and to understand the spiritual essence of human blood requires revelation from the Holy Spirit, not a laboratory and a microscope. We read in Genesis 4:10 that the voice of Abel's blood cried out to God. Well I can hear many of you saying his blood didn't really speak, and that this is just an instance when Scripture utilizes anthropomorphism, which is the act of assigning human characteristics to non-human or inanimate things. My answer to that is since the life of the body is in the blood, the very essence of our humanity is contained in our blood, and beloved it doesn't get more human than that. But that's not the end of the story. James 1:26 (Amplified Bible) says *"For as the human body apart from the spirit is lifeless, so faith apart from [its] works of obedience is dead."* Now if the life of the body is in the blood (Leviticus 17:11), and the human body apart from the spirit is lifeless (dead), then of necessity human blood must contain spiritual life. I am convinced that it was the spiritual life in Abel's blood that raised its voice unto God because that which is not seen (i.e. spiritual) is eternal (2 Corinthians 4:18).

The Hebrew word for blood is dam (pronounced **dawm**) and the first time this word is used in Scripture is in the description of Abel's blood. The unique thing about Adam (pronounced aw-**dawm**), meaning mankind, is that he possessed a substance called blood (**dawm**), which was of such a nature that it sustained natural life in his human body and also sustained his spiritual life, i.e., his connection to and oneness with God as God's son (Luke 3:38). When Adam sinned, the spiritual life present in his blood was removed and he entered into spiritual death. He was still a spirit being, but now he was spiritually dead because he was no longer connected to the source of spiritual life. His biological life wasn't impacted because he was still inhaling and exhaling; nor was his soul life affected because he was still using his intellect, demonstrating emotion, and exercising his will. The only thing that was affected was the life that was of utmost importance, his connection with the source of spiritual life, God Almighty.

Adam's blood was now polluted, and as such, he became susceptible to things that God never intended for mankind to experience, such as sickness, poverty, and death. A litmus test to determine if God intended for mankind to experience a particular thing in the earth realm is if the Scriptures reveal its existence in heaven. It's rather mind-boggling to me that Christians actually believe that a loving and merciful

53

God and Father would keep them poor, make them sick, and eventually kill them. We would call that child abuse! Beloved, I certainly hope you are not in that company. These things are part of the curse and Christ redeemed us from the curse so that we can live the blessed life (Galatians 3:13-14). Settle this in your heart and mind once and for all; God can't give you something that He doesn't have. The Apostle James, the Lord's brother, said it like this: *"Do not err, my beloved brethren. Every good gift and every perfect gift is from above, and cometh down from the Father of lights, with whom is no variableness, neither shadow of turning. Of His own will He begat us with the word of truth, that we should be a kind of firstfruits of his creatures"* (James 1:16-18). If it's not good, and it's not perfect, it didn't come from God as its source. God is always the same. He can't give you something good one day and something bad the next. If He did, he would be inconsistent in character, proven to be a liar and someone we couldn't trust.

It is important to understand that as the result of spiritual death entering into the human family the earth became subject to the curse (Genesis 3:17, see also Deuteronomy 28). Consequently, spiritual forces of darkness gained power over mankind as long as he (mankind) remained separated and alienated from God. Beloved, it is essential that you be especially mindful of the truth that these spiritual forces of darkness (demons) are bent on establishing misery, suffering, and death as preeminent components of our time spent on this people planet (John 10:10; Mark 5). Whoever yields to the influence of these malignant spiritual forces will in turn incur what they have to give, which is destruction. In light of the reality that bad things do happen as a part of our human experience in the earth, it's imperative that we understand the reason why they happen and the source of these experiences. Beloved, they are directly attributable to the fall of man; to the fact that mankind became separated from God as the result of Adam's rebellion. The life and light that was coursing through Adam's body was now transformed into death and darkness, and as his offspring we inherited his dark, demented nature, a nature that Scripture refers to as the flesh.

God Values Life

As the source of life, God places significance on all life, but preeminent value on human life, because in all creation mankind is unique in that they are the only facet of God's creation that is created in His image and His likeness. Having said that, I feel it important to interject that even though some humans have completely given themselves over to darkness and evil, they are still created in God's image and likeness. God hates the sin and what it does to human lives, but He eternally loves the human, the one He created for fellowship with Himself. Anyone who names the name of Christ must commit to valuing and loving every human being. According to 1 Corinthians 13:7 *"Love bears up under anything and everything that comes, is ever ready to believe the best of every person..."* (Amplified Bible, emphasis mine). Wow! I imagine this is a good place to say like Jesus' disciples did; "Lord, increase our faith."

Blood and Covenant

Blood is the source of life and God has declared that for guilty life to be reconciled to Him, innocent life (blood) is the price that must be paid. Hebrews 9:22 (Amplified Bible) says *"[In fact] under the Law almost everything is purified by means of blood, and without the shedding of blood there is neither release from sin and its guilt nor the remission of the due and merited punishment for sins."* In any discussion regarding blood and its place in God's economy (meaning God's rule and His way of doing things) it is important to understand covenant. I ask you, the reader, to indulge me as I try to paint as clear a picture as I possibly can with reference to covenant.

First and foremost, covenant is God's idea. God's plan was (and still is) for man to experience unbroken, eternal fellowship and communion with Him. Even after the fall, God continued to reach out to mankind and encouraged them to live life God's way. God knew that because man's nature had changed, the spiritual life necessary to maintain the connection with Him was no longer abiding within man. As time passed, it is evident according to Scripture, that mankind became woefully aware of this reality as well. But God had an eternal plan that He would play out on the stage of human history. Hallelujah!

God desired that all men would serve Him and be in right relationship with Him, thus the original covenant with mankind was with Adam. After sin entered in, man became exceedingly sinful to the point where God decided to (seemingly) wipe them all off the face of the earth (see Genesis 6:5-7). Scripture records that Noah found grace in God's eyes because Noah walked with God. In other words there was a representative man who determined to do things God's way, who was a descendant of the original covenant partner of God, Adam.

I won't rehearse the account of the flood as I am going to assume that any reader of this book has some level of familiarity with it. What I will point out is that after the flood waters subsided and the ground was dry enough for them to leave the ark, Noah offered a blood sacrifice to reaffirm the covenant between God and man (Genesis 8:20), thus indicating his awareness that blood was the only way to reconciliation and oneness with God. Fundamental to the concept of covenant is that after it is ratified the parties to the covenant become one, and in God's economy, the only substance suitable for sealing an everlasting covenant is blood. Consequently, the covenant partners are not allowed to consider what they possess as exclusively theirs, but now each party to the covenant has an equal claim on everything possessed by the other party. Thus, to be in covenant, or one with God, means that everything that belongs to God now belongs to His covenant partner, and vice-versa. Hallelujah! That is why God gave Noah and his sons the same instructions He gave Adam and Eve relative to their role in the earth realm; to be fruitful, multiply, replenish the earth, and subdue it;

indicating that mankind's role in carrying out God's eternal plan hadn't changed. Whatever God would do in the earth realm He would do through His covenant partner(s). What a gracious and merciful God is the God of heaven & earth!

As the earth became re-populated (Genesis 9-11) God unceasingly reached out to man in order to honor the covenant with Adam but man continually resisted. Man indeed was of the flesh, totally dominated by sin. The epitome of the effects of man's rebellion against God is seen in Genesis 11:1-4 as men united in their effort to construct the Tower of Babel. Within these verses man's intention to live a life free from God's lordship is revealed. Conversely, on a positive note, the awesome creative ability that God imparts into every human being as well as the extraordinary potential present in unity is revealed. God Himself declared that because the people were unified in word and deed (strife was nonexistent among them), nothing would be impossible for them to accomplish. Alas, because man continually rebelled against God, He determined that He would reach out to an individual as opposed to the masses, and through that individual's blood line bring restoration to the masses. Remember, God's plan always has been and always will be that all humanity be in right relationship with Him for all eternity (see 1Timothy 2:4 and 2 Peter 3:9)

Abrahamic Covenant

Hence God appeared to a man named Abram who lived in Ur, which at the time was a thriving metropolis and center of commerce in southern Mesopotamia (modern-day Iraq), and made some extraordinary promises to him, the fulfillment of which was contingent upon Abram walking in obedience to God (Genesis11- 12). In order to achieve this, God required Abram to get away from everyone and everything that would influence him to cling to his previous lifestyle, which was grounded in idol worship. History suggests that he probably worshiped the Babylonian moon god.[vi]

I suppose that this encounter with the living God was pretty intense, life-changing in fact, as it motivated Abram to depart from the familiarity and comfort of what had by all indications become, according to the world's standards, a very prosperous and productive life. Yes, this encounter convinced Abram, who was now 75 years old, that this God who was now revealing Himself was indeed the God above all gods, the true and living God, and that He had so much more to offer than the gods of Abram's fathers. Consequently, Abram took God up on His offer to follow Him and serve Him, not knowing where it would lead or what it would entail, but confident that it was the right choice to make (Genesis 12:4).

So Abram departed from all he had ever known with no specific destination in sight. Because of this, it might appear to the casual observer that Abram was acting on blind faith. Beloved, be assured of one thing...true faith, faith that is alive and vibrant, is never, ever blind. God does not require nor expect us to have blind faith. What He does require is that we trust and act on His word. Abram was armed with and emboldened by God's promise that He would reveal to him the land that was divinely appointed to him, that He would make of Abram a great nation, that He would bless him, make his name great, and make him a blessing. As if that wasn't sufficient, God promised to bless any and every one that blessed Abram, and to curse any and every one that cursed him, and to bless every family on the face of the earth through him (Genesis 12:2-3). What exceeding great and precious promises!

In Genesis chapter 12 through chapter 22 we are privileged to have a ringside seat and observe the evolution of

Abram's walk with God, as well as the progressive manner in which God fulfilled His promise to Abram by ratifying the covenant in stages. Though several covenants are revealed within the pages of the Old Testament (Noahic, Mosaic, Davidic), special emphasis is placed on the Abrahamic covenant as it is the one that is the initial basis for man being restored to right relationship with God. Walk with me as I encapsulate this process and conclude this chapter by confirming that "we need a blood transfusion."

I am of the opinion that except for Jesus, Abram (who later became Abraham) is the most significant individual that ever walked the earth. He is revealed in Scripture as the father through whose natural bloodline the Savior of all humanity would come, as well as being the father of all who would by faith receive the Savior into their lives resulting in their being born into the family of God (Romans 4:12-16; Galatians 3:29). In addition to his faith, I am astounded by the extraordinary courage that Abraham consistently demonstrated. It takes undaunted courage to walk by faith (2 Corinthians 5:7). Anyone who is otherwise minded is someone who is not living by faith in God. The world has been infiltrated by Satan and his minions and everything they stand for is anti-God and anti-Christ. Consequently, anything and everything that represents God in this realm is the target of continual (and frequently violent) opposition. It takes extreme courage to stand up to and overcome this opposition.

Imagine for a moment the opposition Abram must have encountered, not only in his own thought processes, but from his family as well. Remember, polytheism, which is the worship of many gods, was all they had ever known. I'm sure his wife and others close to him must have thought he had lost his mind! I can envision Sarai, Abram's wife, pulling out all the stops to get him to reconsider his decision. Needless to say her efforts were futile. Abram had a defining experience with the living God which laid the foundation for his faith while simultaneously fueling his faith. This experience provided the parameters for how he would keep his life on the proper course to walk into divine destiny, just as the banks of a river keep it on course to arrive at its appointed destination.

So Abram and his clan arrived in the land of Canaan to begin their new life. Based on the promise given him by God, it's reasonable to assume Abram was confident that everything would be smooth sailing. Wrong! It was anything but smooth sailing. The people in this new land were jealous of him and didn't like him. One of the kings of the land tried to take Abram's wife into his harem. He had to deal with a family feud between his workers and his nephew's workers. To make matters worse he had to rescue his nephew (Lot) and five kings along with their subjects, and in his effort to remain faithful to God, he refused a significant material reward from the King of Sodom (see Genesis 14:22-24). None of the promises God made to him had come to pass yet and I can imagine Abram began to wonder himself if he'd made a terribly bad decision by leaving the comfortable life he knew in exchange for what he was now experiencing. To his credit, in spite of the extraordinarily daunting challenges with which he had been bombarded, Abram hung in there and kept standing on the word he received from the Lord.

God's Faithfulness

God, in His faithfulness, made sure Abram's faithfulness wouldn't go unrewarded. Yes beloved, God rewards faithfulness (see Matthew 25:21)! Genesis 15:1 (NET) records the following: *After these things, the word of the Lord came to Abram in a vision: "Fear not, Abram! I am your shield and the one who will reward you in great abundance."* God assured Abram that his repeated sacrifices were absolutely worth it because Abram got the greatest reward of all...**he got God!**

In light of everything Abram experienced following his decision to walk with God, it's easy to understand why, that in spite of this glorious proclamation by God, he still had some trust issues. Abram responded to God by essentially saying "I hear you talking God but how do I know you really mean what you say and you aren't just toying with me?" Then God gave him a seemingly bizarre instruction...He told Abram to go get a cow! Now to those of us whose thinking has been shaped by the postmodern Western worldview we would probably be convinced that God had just flipped His lid! Not Abram though. In fact, he probably started leaping and dancing and shouting for joy. In ancient Eastern culture covenants were frequently entered into by slaying a cow, dividing it in two and placing the halves opposite each other, pouring the blood that was shed by the animal between the two halves, and the parties to the covenant would walk together through the blood that was between the pieces in order to seal the covenant.[vii] The cutting in halves of the sacrifice signified the end of the existing lives for the sake of establishing a new bond or covenant. Abram realized that God was preparing to allow Himself to be bound by the terms of a covenant agreement, which in essence was an agreement that if not fulfilled by either party, the injured party had the legal right to kill the other party to the covenant and their subsequent generations. Well certainly Abram couldn't kill God, but God could absolutely annihilate Abram if he didn't honor the terms of the covenant.

Covenant Ratification

But a strange thing happened. Genesis 15:17-18 (Amplified Bible) records it like this: *"When the sun had gone down and a [thick] darkness had come on, behold a smoking oven and a flaming torch passed between those pieces. On the same day the Lord made a covenant (promise, pledge) with Abram, saying, To your descendants I have given this land, from the river of Egypt to the great river Euphrates..."* Abram never passed through the pieces to seal the covenant. The smoking oven and flaming torch was God Himself passing through the pieces and assuming full responsibility for keeping the covenant by honoring His promises. [viii] Abram's responsibility was to believe that God would do everything He promised. Genesis 15:6 (Amplified Bible) states in reference to Abram: *"And he [Abram] believed in (trusted in, relied on, remained steadfast to) the Lord, and He counted it to him as righteousness (right standing with God)."* This initial ratification of the covenant most likely occurred when Abram was somewhere between the ages of 84 and 86. It was called a royal grant and God promised that the land falling within the boundaries He described would forever belong to Abram and his descendants after him. That land is modern-day Israel.

In Genesis 17, God appears to Abram again, thirteen years after the previously recorded interaction, and reaffirms the covenant and promises Abram that in his old age (100) he would father a child that his wife Sarai in her old age (90) would bear. At this time God changed Abram's name to his covenant name of Abraham and Sarai's name to her covenant name of Sarah. It was also at this time that God instituted the rite of circumcision of all the male descendants in Abraham's lineage and the servants in his household as the external sign of the covenant relationship. There was a dual symbolism in this act. First, it was a constant reminder that in order to walk with God there must be a cutting away of the flesh (see Romans 8:8). Additionally, the cutting away of the male foreskin of course resulted in blood flow, and that blood symbolically would be on the seed of all those in covenant relationship with God. This was a reminder that blood was necessary to be restored to right relationship with God.

Just as God promised, Sarah conceived and bore a son (Genesis 21). What joy and exultation Abraham and Sarah must have experienced at the manifestation of the promised child. He was certainly named appropriately, for Isaac means laughter. I imagine that when they rehearsed how illogical it was for them to be parents at their age, they probably started laughing and didn't stop for a long time. They experienced first-hand that with God nothing is impossible (Luke 1:37).

Let's fast-forward to Genesis chapter 22. The previous chapter ends by stating that **"Abraham sojourned in the Philistines' land many days."** One can infer that since the Scripture makes no mention of any dramatic events following this statement that Abraham's, Sarah's, and Isaac's time in this land was for the most part unremarkable. It certainly wouldn't be far-fetched to believe that they were enjoying God's blessing, enjoying each other, and enjoying life.

The Sacrifice that Covenant Required

Then, just when they thought it was safe to go back in the water (forgive my poor attempt at humor), God starts talking again; and He had something to say that Abraham probably hadn't anticipated. Scripture records the interaction as follows: *After all this, God tested Abraham. God said, "Abraham!" "Yes?" answered Abraham. "I'm listening." He said, "Take your dear son Isaac whom you love and go to the land of Moriah. Sacrifice him there as a burnt offering on one of the mountains that I'll point out to you"* (Genesis 22:1-2 The Message). Wow! I have, on more than one occasion, tried to imagine what it must have been like to receive that instruction from God. Certainly, in the point in time that we exist, our societal structure wouldn't permit such an act; therefore I'm pretty confident God wouldn't require us to carry out such a deed. Nevertheless, trying to wrap my brain around obeying such a command is, to put it mildly, overwhelming.

Genesis 22:3-5 (The Message) states *"Abraham got up early in the morning and saddled his donkey. He took two of his young servants and his son Isaac. He had split wood for the burnt offering. He set out for the place God had directed him. On the third day he looked up and saw the place in the distance. Abraham told his two young servants, 'Stay here with the donkey. The boy and I are going over there to worship; then we'll come back to you'."* In reading this passage it would be easy to assume that Abraham put a great big smile on his face, told God he would respond to His command right away, and went to bed and had a terrific night's sleep; arising full of energy and ready to sacrifice his son. I contend that what he experienced was exactly the opposite of what I just described. I can see Abraham agonizing through the night, wrestling with his willingness to continue to obey God. I would even liken it, to a small degree, with what Jesus experienced in Gethsemane, in that Abraham had to come to the place where his faith enabled him to become resolute in carrying out God's expressed will, no matter what the personal cost. Remember, he was instructed to shed the blood (thereby sacrificing the life) of the son whom he loved! What great faith this must have required! What great respect for and commitment to the covenant relationship he had with God! What a tremendous display of his love for the Lord! Abraham, when confronted with what was most likely the greatest faith test he would ever encounter, determined that he was going the distance with God, leaving us an example that no matter the circumstance, we can obey God!

As Abraham was in the act of sacrificing his son an angel stopped him before he could consummate the act. The encounter is recorded as follows: *"Abraham reached out and took the knife to kill his son. Just then an angel of God called to him out of Heaven, 'Abraham! Abraham!' 'Yes, I'm listening.' Don't lay a hand on that boy! Don't touch him! Now I know how fearlessly you fear God; you didn't hesitate to place your son, your dear son, on the altar for me"* (Genesis 22:10-12 The Message).

Here's why all of this is significant. The Abrahamic covenant is the model for the New Covenant. In both covenants God Almighty takes responsibility for their fulfillment. To enter into the aforementioned covenants, the other party to the covenant need only believe that God will do what He promised to do (see Genesis 15:6; Acts 16:31; & Romans 4:23-25). Abraham, having very clear insight into the seriousness of the blood covenant, understood that as God's covenant partner he was bound to surrender to God whatever He required. Consequently, he knew that his possessions were no longer his own but that his covenant partner, in this case God, had an equal claim on everything that belonged to him. Likewise, through the blood covenant, God proclaimed to the entire universe that Abraham had an equal claim to everything that belonged to Him, which is everything in creation. I recognize that this is a mind-boggling pronouncement but two becoming one is the very essence of covenant.

So God laid claim to the very thing that was nearest and dearest to Abraham's heart...He asked Abraham to give to Him the son whom he loved very much. The initial thought that probably comes to mind is how could God, the God who is love personified, do such a thing? I know from personal experience, and maybe you can testify to this as well, the feeling of reluctance that would come upon me when God required me to give to Him things that were near and dear to me. Maybe it was a sum of money that I had other plans for, or the relinquishing of my own right to be right in order to maintain peace, or even a habit that I had grown very fond of and had no desire to let go. In the final analysis, the only legitimate response for one who is in relationship with the living God is "yes Lord!"

The Reward of Covenant Sacrifice

Abraham recognized that his only options were to either honor the sanctity of the blood covenant or disregard it. Understanding covenant the way that he did, the only real choice for Abraham was to comply with his covenant part-ner's request. Hebrews 11:17-19 provides us with insight into Abraham's thought process throughout this ordeal. It reads as follows: *"By faith Abraham, when he was put to the test [while the testing of his faith was still in progress], had already brought Isaac for an offering; he who had gladly received and welcomed [God's] promises was ready to sacrifice his only son, Of whom it was said, Through Isaac shall your descendants be reckoned. For he reasoned that God was able to raise [him] up even from the dead. Indeed in the sense that Isaac was figuratively dead [potentially sacrificed], he did [actually] receive him back from the dead"* (Amplified Bible). Abraham stood on God's promise and was confident that what God had promised he was able (and willing) to perform. He was fully persuaded that his descendants would come through Isaac based on what God promised him; so if it meant Isaac had to be raised from the dead to accomplish that …then so be it!

Beloved, the beauty and wonder of Abraham being faithful to the blood covenant was this; because Abraham, as the one through whom God promised all nations would be blessed, offered his son to God, God, because of the unilateral covenant he bound Himself by, was obligated to sacrifice his Son for all humanity. Hallelujah! Because Abraham was willing to shed the blood of his son Isaac (remember that life is in the blood), God could now legally allow His

Son's blood to be shed for the sins of many. Hallelujah! How far beyond natural comprehension is the wisdom of God!

As you are well aware, this chapter is entitled "We Need a Blood Transfusion." This is the case because sin created the necessity for mankind to be restored to right relationship with God. The only way for this separation to be remedied was for innocent life (blood) to be sacrificed for guilty (sinful) life. Isaiah 53:10-11 (NLT) states: *"But it was the Lord's good plan to crush him and cause him grief. Yet when his life is made an offering for sin, he will have many descendants. He will enjoy a long life and the Lord's good plan will prosper in his hands. When he sees all that is accomplished by his anguish, he will be satisfied. And because of his experience, my righteous servant will make it possible for many to be counted righteous, for he will bear all their sins."*

To transfuse means to transfer or pass from one to another; to diffuse into or through; and to permeate.[ix] Right standing with God and restoration to our original state has as its fundamental component the shedding of blood and the concept of covenant. The only way this becomes effectual for any individual is for them to willingly appropriate what God has done. It is necessary for us to receive God's life, which is inherent in the shed blood of Jesus. Jesus stated

*"This cup is the new covenant between God and his people –
an agreement confirmed with my blood, which is poured out
as a sacrifice for you"* (Luke 22:20 NLT). By appropriating
what the shed blood of Jesus accomplished, the life of God
is transfused throughout our human spirit and we become
one with God, hence *"the person who is joined to the Lord is
one spirit with him"* (1 Corinthians 6:17 NLT). Hallelujah!
Glory to God forevermore!

Chapter 5

Restoration

But the father said to his servants, Bring quickly the best robe (the festive robe of honor) and put it on him; and give him a ring for his hand and sandals for his feet. And bring out that [wheat-]fattened calf and kill it; and let us revel and feast and be happy and make merry, Because this my son was dead and is alive again; he was lost and is found! And they began to revel and feast and make merry (Luke 15:22-24 Amplified Bible).

The Beauty of Restoration

*A*masterpiece is considered to be an individual's greatest and most prolific piece of work, and is accomplished through masterly skill, intense focus, extraordinary attention to detail, unwavering discipline, and, of course, unbridled creativity. If you've lived on this planet long enough you've probably heard reports of art collectors or museums incurring what many would consider inordinate financial expense to obtain what the art world categorizes as a masterpiece. The beauty of the object provides the careful observer with a peek into the artist's soul, and causes the imagination to run wild envisioning how the process of producing such beauty must have impacted its creator. Consequently, the observer is left overwhelmed with amazement, awe, and appreciation for the artist's giftedness and passion. Were such a treasure to incur any damage that marred its original splendor, it would in all likelihood, elicit the sparing of no expense by those who had been impacted by its magnificence to restore it to its original beauty and grandeur. Once restored, those impacted by its initial opulence frequently experience an even a greater appreciation for the masterpiece.

Beloved, mankind always has been, currently is, and always will be God's ultimate masterpiece. Reducing this statement to its lowest terms...**YOU ARE GOD'S MASTERPIECE!** You've probably heard the statement "God don't make no junk!" In spite of the poor grammar associated with that statement, no truer words have ever been spoken. Scripture bears this out because after surveying His creation, God didn't say it was "very good" until after His masterpiece was completed (Genesis 1:31). God is so enamored by mankind, so appreciative of the regal demeanor that He bestowed upon man, so captivated by the beauty of His premier creation, that He rejoices over you with singing (Zephaniah 3:17). In light of this, it is easy to understand God's extreme displeasure when His masterpiece became marred by the repugnance and degradation that sin produced, as well as His willingness to take whatever measures were necessary to restore His creation to its original majesty and glory.

This is an appropriate place to interject that it is absolutely essential that we have the right concept of who God is. Frequently He is portrayed as an austere, unreasonably rigid being that is just looking for any opportunity to punish us. There is also the perception that God is this distant and absent God who has left us to figure things out on our own. That is not who God is! He is a gracious, merciful, loving, and ever-present God and Father who is infinitely interested in and committed to our highest good. I mention this because our perception of God greatly influences how (or if) we respond to Him.

People frequently relegate God's grace to being a New Testament phenomenon, but nothing could be further from the truth. God is always the same. So if He was gracious in New Testament times He was gracious prior to them. Jesus is the Lamb slain from the foundation of the world (Revelation 13:8). Since He is the one through whom God's amazing grace is made manifest for all to behold and receive, in the mind of God this grace was available in abundant measure before there was an actual need for it in time and space. What an awesome God He is! He is truly worthy of the worship of all humanity! Scripture informs us that *"God shows and clearly proves His [own] love for us by the fact that while we were still sinners, Christ (the Messiah, the Anointed One) died for us* (Romans 5:8 Amplified Bible); and *"He who did not withhold or spare [even] His own Son but gave Him up for us all, will He not also with Him freely and graciously give us all [other] things"* (Romans 8:32 Amplified Bible)? My friend, this affirms that God spared no expense in order to restore His masterpiece to its original kingly estate.

Having interacted in Christian circles for a little over twenty years, fourteen of them as an ordained minister of the gospel, I have seen and heard many things. One such thing is the manner in which many believers view redemption. In my experience, there is a disproportionate propensity to view redemption exclusively through the lens of what we are saved from to the omission or marginalization of considering what we are saved to. In other words many express their thankfulness that the penalty for sin has been satisfied and eternal damnation is not in their future; but relative to what we are saved to, they only consider, to coin a phrase, "the great by and by," as opposed to including what is ours right now. Fundamental to the concept of restoration is the here and now. Consider this, if you lose something valuable are you content to wait an indefinite amount of time to have it restored to you or do you desire it to be restored right here and right now?

In chapter 15 of Luke's gospel, the common theme is restoration; restoration of the lost sheep, restoration of the lost coin, and restoration of the lost son. Though there is an overarching theme among each circumstance, there is a significant difference in how restoration is accomplished in the case of the lost son. In the first two instances the owner of the lost item exerted tremendous effort in searching for the lost item, and upon locating it, they rejoiced greatly. But with the son, everything the father had was available to him without restriction. Yet, he chose to walk away from the security of the father's house in exchange for what he was deceived into thinking was a better proposition. The father, in his unconditional love, maintained a place in his heart, and his home, for the lost son. But because the son willingly left, the only way for restoration to occur was for the son to willingly return to the love and security of the father's home.

Upon the son's return, the father took very specific actions, none of which were without significance. In case you didn't know, the Lord Jesus told this parable to depict God the Father's response to the return of the lost son and His commitment to the son's total restoration, with the son being representative of all humanity. The father didn't condemn the previously wayward son upon his return and didn't even want to discuss his act of rebellion. Ultimately, it didn't matter to the father what the son had done. All that mattered was that the son took advantage of the father's provision for him to return to where he rightfully belonged.

The first action the father took was to place the best robe in the house upon the repentant son. This custom was symbolic and reserved for the guest of honor in ancient Middle Eastern homes. As an action of the father, it is indicative of the son being restored to his original honor and dignity. Next, the father had his servants place the family ring on his finger. In biblical times the family ring was typically a signet ring with the family name or seal on it and indicated that the wearer of the ring had the authority to handle the affairs of the family. Lastly, the father commanded that sandals be placed on the son's feet. Slaves typically went barefoot and this action was the culmination of the son's restoration, indicating that what had previously reduced him to his low estate no longer had any power over him. He was now, and forever, free from the past. No more regrets, no more sorrow, no more fear; only immersion into the total restoration to his previously high estate and kingly dignity. HALLELUJAH!

Through the blood of Jesus, the blood of the everlasting covenant (Hebrews 13:20), our redemption is complete. Nothing can be added to it. We are restored to the original state of affairs. Our inheritance as sons is restored to us, completely and eternally! Romans 8:17 (NLT) states *"And since we are his children, we are his heirs. In fact, together with Christ we are heirs of God's glory."* Take a moment and consider the import of this verse of Scripture. We inherit God's glory, both now and forever! According to 2 Corinthians 5:17(Amplified Bible) *"Therefore if any person* is *[ingrafted] in Christ (the Messiah) he is a new creation (a new creature altogether); the old [previous moral and spiritual condition] has passed away. Behold, the fresh and new has come."*

Yes indeed, through our union with Jesus we are a new creature altogether. New in the sense that we are able to experience a reality that sin previously prohibited us from knowing in time and space. In actuality, in the mind of God, relative to the purpose of his premier creation, his masterpiece, it is not necessarily new but the consummation of the restoration to its original condition. And as God and all creation steadfastly observe the effect of the restoration, once again, they have a profound appreciation and regard for the beauty God's masterpiece possesses, and are overjoyed by the pleasure they derive as a result. This is why we are informed that *"For [even the whole] creation (all nature) waits expectantly and longs earnestly for God's sons to be made known [waits for the revealing, the disclosing of their sonship]"* (Romans 8:19 Amplified Bible). Beloved, this is referring to all who will accept the responsibility that accompanies being a son of God. Hopefully, this is referring to you.

Chapter 6

Who are the Sons of God?

෧෨

But as many as received him, to them gave he power to become the sons of God, even to them that believe on his name: Which were born, not of blood, nor of the will of the flesh, nor of the will of man, but of God (John 1:12-13)... *Now I say, That the heir, as long as he is a child, differeth nothing from a servant, though he be lord of all; But is under tutors and governors until the time appointed of the father... And because ye are sons, God has sent forth the Spirit of his Son into your hearts, crying, Abba, Father. Wherefore thou art no more a servant, but a son; and if a son, then an heir of God through Christ* (Galatians 4:1-2; 6-7).

*W*hat an extraordinary privilege to be a member of the royal family of God. How amazing it is to be a son of God! The Apostle John must have been contemplating this very reality when the Holy Spirit inspired him to pen the following words: *"Behold, what manner of love the father bestowed upon us, that we should be called the sons of God: therefore the world knoweth us not, because it knew him not. Beloved, now are we the sons of God, and it doth not yet appear what we shall be: but we know that, when he shall appear, we shall be like him; for we shall see him as he is. And every man that hath this hope in him purifieth himself, even as he is pure"* (1John 3:1-3).

Something that typically happens in the process of translation is that some of the nuances of the original language are lost. In reading the way the word sons is used in each of the preceding passages, one would think that they all mean the same thing, but that is not the case. As you may or may not know, the New Testament was originally written in "Koine" (pronounced ko-nay) or common Greek. Greek is a very exact language and in the New Testament there are two primary Greek words that are translated as the English word son(s). They are teknon (pronounced **tek**-non) and huios (pronounced hwee-**os).** The word teknon is used when describing external characteristics related to sonship, essentially used to denote birth and identify lineage. It is probably best translated by using the word children. The word huios is used to describe the mature son, one who has demonstrated their readiness to assume responsibility for the father's inheritance. This term emphasizes the dignity and character of the relationship between father and son. The term huios is the only word the New Testament uses in reference to Jesus.

According to 1John 2:6 (Amplified Bible), *"Whoever says he abides in Him ought [as a personal debt] to walk and conduct himself in the same way in which He walked and conducted Himself."* Wow! This is actually saying that we owe it to God to live our lives in the earth the same way that Jesus did, that is to say, as one who has demonstrated that they are mature enough to handle the Father's inheritance and fulfill God's purpose. Well, what does that mean in actual practice? To begin with, if we are going to be replicas of Jesus the Christ (Christian actually means one who is a follower of and hence like Christ) we need to understand what He came to do, and then just do it.

Jesus the Christ is the incarnate will of God, the incarnate obedience, Who works in us what God wrought in Him. Christ came as the Son of God, to impart to us the very same life and disposition that governed Him on earth. First and foremost, Jesus proclaimed that *"My food (nourishment) is*

*to do the will (pleasure) of Him Who sent Me and to accom-
plish and completely finish His work"* (John 4:34 Amplified
Bible). This is what is at the heart of mature sonship, doing
the Father's will and advancing the Father's interests. Please
understand, the carrying out of the Father's will should not
be out of compulsion, but the fruit of a mutual love relationship...the Father eternally loving us unconditionally, and our
response to His love. Love seeks not its own but desires to
please and bless the object of its love (1Corinthians 13:5).
Additionally, by His own testimony, Jesus declared that He
came to give us life (literally life as God has it) in the most
abundant measure (John 10:10), and to seek and to save that
which is lost (Luke 19:10). The Holy Spirit adds in 1John
3:8 (Amplified Bible) *"...The reason the Son of God was
made manifest (visible) was to undo (destroy, loosen, and
dissolve) the works the devil [has done]."*

Make no mistake, even though God is not a respecter of
persons, He certainly differentiates between who He entrusts
to accomplish His purposes. Proverbs 25:19 (NLT) declares
***"Putting confidence in an unreliable person in times of
trouble is like chewing with a broken tooth or walking on
a lame foot."*** Anyone who has encountered either of these
situations knows firsthand just how problematic and painful

they can be, and how they prohibit the accomplishment of their designated purpose.

In Jewish culture when the son reaches a certain age he has a bar mitzvah, which is a public pronouncement and celebration that the son has reached the place in their life where the father is willing to trust him with the father's inheritance. Much study, training, and preparation goes into helping the son arrive at this momentous occasion in his life. It is indicative of how serious and intentional God is about his plans and purposes coming to pass, and how He will only entrust this responsibility to those who have demonstrated their preparedness to handle it. Don't get me wrong, God loves everyone who has been born into His family by appropriating the finished work of Jesus, but we determine what God entrusts to us by our ever-increasing display of devotion to accomplishing the Father's will. Even if God has spoken to your heart about the great things He wants you to accomplish, it won't happen if you remain a babe in Christ.

The Apostle Paul informs the Corinthian church *"But the natural, nonspiritual man does not accept or welcome or admit into his heart the gifts and teachings and revelations of the Spirit of God, for they are folly (meaningless nonsense) to him; and he is incapable of knowing them [of progressively recognizing, understanding, and becoming better acquainted with them] because they are spiritually discerned and estimated and appreciated"*... *"However, Brethren, I could not talk to you as to spiritual [men], but as to nonspiritual [men of the flesh, in whom the carnal nature predominates], as to mere infants [in the new life] in Christ [unable to talk yet!] I fed you with milk, not solid food, for you were not yet strong enough [to be ready for it]; but even yet you are not strong enough [to be ready for it], For you are still [unspiritual, having the nature] of the flesh [under the control of ordinary impulses]... behaving your-selves after a human standard and like mere (unchanged) men"* (1Corinthians 2:14; 3:1-3 Amplified Bible). Now of course this applies to unbelievers, i.e., those who haven't received Jesus as their Savior and Lord, but the Apostle Paul wasn't speaking to unbelievers. He was speaking to those who had made a public profession that Jesus was their Lord. Hence, it can be inferred that just as this Scripture applies to unbelievers, it applies equally to carnal Christians, those who for whatever reason, don't mature in their walk with God. They are still a part of the family and objects of God's immense love, but God deals with them just like any parent deals with a baby. Because they haven't demonstrated the desire to mature in their faith, they aren't entrusted with much responsibility.

Here's a little food for thought. We will spend tens, sometimes hundreds of thousands of dollars to prepare us to succeed in the world, but many believers won't even consider investing five hundred dollars to better prepare themselves to fulfill God's purpose for their lives.

In the Scripture reference from Galatians that I used to introduce this chapter, it is clear that as long as the child of God remains a babe they will not be able to experience the fullness of everything God has for them while they remain in the earth. Someone will have to assume responsibility for their inheritance until such time as they consistently demonstrate to God they can handle it themselves. It's the same concept as the trustee of an estate. Though the full inheritance belongs to the inheritor, they don't have complete access to it. It must be doled out based on the specific instructions of the grantor, or in the case of death, the testator, until such time as the inheritor reaches the age of majority, or sometimes beyond that. It's important to know my friend, that God doesn't base suitability and preparedness to handle his inheritance on chronological age. He bases it solely on spiritual maturity. You can be eighty years old and still in second grade spiritually because God doesn't buy into the notion of social promotion. If you want to get out of the spiritual second grade you have to successfully pass the spiritual tests at that level.

Beloved of God, it has absolutely nothing to do with how much God loves you. Consider this, how willing would you be to entrust something of extraordinary value and significance to someone who has yet demonstrated their readiness to handle it? Yes that question was rhetorical... and if we have sense enough to know better how can we dare think that God doesn't? Be very clear on this point, being in the family is not equivalent to mature sonship in the Kingdom of God. Sonship denotes an ever-increasing level of spiritual maturity. Sonship reveals one's willingness to grow up and have as its main focus the accomplishing of the Father's will and the advancing of the Father's kingdom.

So who are the sons of God? They are those who love the Lord our God with all their, heart, mind, soul, and strength and love their neighbors (i.e., all humanity) as themselves. They are those who comprehend that everything that was lost by the actions of the first Adam is completely restored to and available for us by the actions of the last Adam (Jesus). They are those who are as comfortable accessing their spiritual inheritance and operating in the supernatural sphere as they are the natural sphere. The sons of God are those who recognize, understand, and esteem the great privilege and responsibility that comes with being entrusted with the "keys to the kingdom of heaven" (Matthew 16:19). The sons of God are those who take up the charge to pray without ceasing, to readily forgive, and for whom worship of the Almighty God is a lifestyle and not relegated to singular events. To be a mature son of God, one must be willing to readily submit to authority in order to exercise the authority with which they have been endowed. The sons of God are those who understand what it means to walk by faith and not by sight and to progressively advance from one level of faith to the next.

The sons of God are those that continually seek the heart of God and understand that holiness means taking on and displaying the attributes and characteristics of a holy God. Sonship means we annihilate the works of the devil and turn the world upside down (Acts 17:6). At the heart of sonship is the desire and ability to continually proclaim "here am I Lord...send me!" Finally, sonship is revealed in and through those who will allow God to use them to fill the earth with His glory, no matter what the personal cost. Beloved, are you a son? If so, all of creation is waiting for you to step up, or go to the next level as the case may be, in the manifestation of your sonship. Yes, if that's you, all of creation is waiting on you (Selah)!

Chapter 7

It's Manifestation Time!

For [even the whole] creation (all nature) waits expectantly and longs earnestly for God's sons to be made known [waits for the revealing, the disclosing of their sonship]. For the creation (nature) was subjected to frailty (to futility, condemned to frustration), not because of some intentional fault on its part, but by the will of Him Who subjected it— [yet] with the hope That nature (creation) itself will be set free from its bondage to decay and corruption [and gain an entrance] into the glorious freedom of God's children (Romans 8:19-21 Amplified Bible).

*W*e live in an hour where life is happening at break-neck speed and Bible prophecy is continually being fulfilled as each moment passes. As I survey our global community these Holy Ghost inspired words penned by the Apostle Paul ring truer and truer: *"For the time is coming when [people] will not tolerate (endure) sound and wholesome instruction, but, having ears itching[for something pleasing and gratifying], they will gather to themselves one teacher after another to a considerable number, chosen to satisfy their own liking and to foster the errors they hold, And will turn aside from hearing truth and wander off into myths and man-made fictions"* (2Timothy 4:3-4 Amplified Bible). There is a quote that is frequently attributed to Edmund Burke, an Irish political philosopher who lived in the 1700's, and it reads as follows: "All that is necessary for the triumph of evil is that good men do nothing." I contend that evil gains the upper-hand when God's people do nothing, or at least don't do enough.

Jesus is coming back soon! Yes, I know that no man knows the day or hour, but I also know that we are closer to His return today than we were yesterday. If ever there was a time for the church to display their sonship that time is now. One thing that I have become acutely aware of is that people are losing hope. The societal institutions that have historically been stable and trustworthy have failed us in a big way. I believe that is one of the reasons we are beginning to experience myriad atrocities that a few short years ago were considered unthinkable. It is essential for those believers that are sons of God in more than name only to be for a lost, dying, sin-sick world, as I stated in the introduction, everything that God created us to be.

We are the salt of the earth, here to preserve and advance righteousness, justice, and moral purity. We are the light of the world, responsible for showing all humanity the way to live life in a manner that is pleasing to God (Colossians 1:10). I certainly understand there can be a propensity, from an individual standpoint, to be overwhelmed with the numerous ills that confront our society. While it may be unreasonable to expect one individual to reach the entire world, it is certainly not unreasonable to expect an individual to reach their world...their family, their friends, their co-workers, and their neighbors. Yes, it is those in what I will refer to as our intimate circles that are waiting for us to allow God to, through us, love them back to wholeness.

My friend, allow me to take this opportunity to remind you that you and God are an unbeatable combination. Because God is for you it doesn't matter who may try to be against you, because greater is He that is in you than he that is in the world (1John 4:4). As I study Scripture I find that in the midst of various crises facing His people, God frequently used a remnant from within his people to accomplish victory. Gideon started out with 32,000 men but God was able to defeat their foes with only 300 men (Judges 7:1-7). God used one man, the prophet Elijah, to overthrow the tyranny and idolatry of 450 prophets of Baal (1Kings 18:19-40). Abraham defeated four kings and their armies with 318 trained servants (Genesis 14:14-16). God used a handful of believers, comparatively speaking, who were full of faith and emboldened by the Holy Spirit, to turn the world upside (Acts 17:6). The "hall of faith" delineated in Hebrews chapter eleven affirms that the list goes on and on.

Beloved, if you believe that the Bible is true, that it is the inerrant, authoritative word of God, you must acknowledge that the only answer for mankind is Jesus the Christ. Jesus has determined that the church, His body, will be the instrument through which He relieves all that burdens mankind. His desire is that all within the church would arise and assume their position of sonship so that the Father God can entrust the entire church with the proper handling of the Father's business, which is to eliminate the kingdom of darkness and advance the kingdom of God in this realm, permeating the earth with righteousness, peace, and joy in the Holy Spirit (Romans 14:17).

Naturally speaking, for a family unit to function effectively each member of that family must bear a certain level of responsibility. Though the responsibilities may vary in scope, none is without significance. Unfortunately, we've been exposed to so many dysfunctional families that this almost seems to be the norm rather than the exception. Consequently, until each member of a family gets born again by the Spirit of God they will never even have a chance to fulfill God's purpose for that family. Well, in God's family there is no dysfunction. One reason for this is that the kingdom of God is not a democracy but a theocracy. God's word is not open for debate. It is the final answer for every member of His family! In fact, the word of God is the final answer for all humanity, and as the sons of God, we have to fulfill our familial responsibility and help the masses realize it.

I understand all too well the inclination to assume the posture that Gideon, Moses, and Jeremiah the prophet did when they flat out told God that He had the wrong person for the job. Beloved, you are not the wrong person. You are the one God wants to use. You are the one that God wants to bless so that He can bless others through you. In fact, you have come into God's kingdom for such a time as this (Esther 4:14).

God is not interested in what you perceive to be your limited ability; He's only interested in your availability. He has made His supernatural ability readily available to and for all who will access it by faith. Here's a startling revelation... all that you will ever need is in Jesus, and if you have received Him, Jesus is in you (Selah)! Jesus proclaimed that *"...you shall receive power (ability, efficiency, and might) when the Holy Spirit has come upon you* (Acts 1:8 Amplified Bible)! Furthermore, the Holy Spirit by way of the Apostle Paul informs us that God *"...by (in consequence of) the [action of His] power that is at work within us, is able to [carry out His purpose and] do superabundantly, far over and above all that we [dare] ask or think [infinitely beyond our highest prayers, desires, thoughts, hopes, or dreams]"* (Ephesians 3:20 Amplified Bible). What power is he referring to? The same power that God has and exerts which is residing in you through the Holy Spirit. This is supernatural, miraculous, wonder-working, devil-defeating power! But until you access it as a son it will remain dormant.

Beloved, you will never walk in what I have discussed in the preceding pages through your own effort. Your own effort equates to putting confidence in the flesh, and the moment you engage the flesh you bring faith to a screeching halt. In any circumstance faith is inoperative and inactive God won't be found (Romans 14:23; Hebrews 11:6). God provides grace in abundant measure to help us. Yes, grace is God's unmerited favor. We can't earn it and we certainly didn't deserve it. It is the gift of God so we should esteem it highly. This is accomplished by appropriating it. It's essential that we understand that because God favors us He empowers us, thus enabling us to always triumph. That's why Jesus stated to the Apostle Paul when he was at his wit's end; *"My grace (My favor and loving-kindness and mercy) is enough for you [sufficient against any danger and enables you to bear the trouble manfully]; for My strength and power are made perfect (fulfilled and completed) and show themselves most effective in [your] weakness"* (2Corinthians 12:9 Amplified Bible). All you need to do is continually yield to the operation of the Holy Spirit in your life and let Him transform you from a child of God into a son of God, for sonship is indeed your destiny. According to Romans 8:29 (Amplified Bible); *"For those whom He foreknew [of whom He was aware and loved beforehand], He also destined from the beginning [foreordaining them] to be molded into the image of His Son [and share inwardly His likeness], that He might become the firstborn among many brethren."*

We have been appointed to live life in the earth exactly the way Jesus did (John 14:12; 1John 2:6; Ephesians 5:1). The Father beckons for our progression from child (which is the equivalent of servant) to son, one who is well-prepared to handle the Father's business. It is indeed time for the manifestation of the sons of God. Beloved, assume and fulfill your appointed role as son. All of creation is waiting.

ENDNOTES

i.   Enhanced Strong's Lexicon, Woodside Bible Fellowship; Dictionary of Biblical Languages Greek New Testament, Logos Research Systems, Inc.

ii.   Billye Brim, *The Blood and the Glory,* Harrison House Publishers, Tulsa, OK

iii.   Enhanced Strong's Lexicon, Woodside Bible Fellowship; Dictionary of Biblical Languages Greek New Testament, Logos Research Systems, Inc.

iv.   Retrieved from Genetic Home Reference website

v.   Dictionary of Biblical Languages Hebrew Old Testament, Logos Research Systems, Inc.

vi.   Nelson's Illustrated Manners and Customs of the Bible, Thomas Nelson Publishers, Nashville, TN

vii. Spirit Filled Life Study Bible, Thomas Nelson Publishers, Nashville, TN

viii. The Bible Knowledge Commentary, Dallas Theological Seminary

ix.   Merriam -Webster Collegiate Dictionary (Eleventh Edition)

About the Author

❧

*M*cClinton Elliott Porter first confessed Christ during his adolescence and recommitted His life to the Lord as he approached his thirtieth birthday. Following his re-committal, McClinton had an innate desire to become a serious student of God's word and to live life in a manner that would glorify God in every way. Sensing God's leading to prepare for ministry, McClinton enrolled in Bible School at Oral Robert's Midwest School of Theology and Ministry in Tinley Park, IL; earning a Diploma in Theological Studies in 1997. Additionally, McClinton earned his B.S. in Business Administration from Roosevelt University in Chicago, Illinois and his M.S. in Nonprofit Management from Spertus College of Judaica, also in Chicago.

Having a heart for the lost and the disenfranchised, McClinton has been involved in numerous facets of his church's outreach ministries. He regularly ministers the gospel to inmates at the Cook County Jail in Chicago, which he has done since 1994. Professionally, McClinton served as Assistant Executive Director of a community-based nonprofit organization that provided mental health, housing, recreational, and educational services to Chicago's at-risk inner city youth. Currently, McClinton ministers at various churches throughout the Chicago area and also provides consultation for nonprofit organizations and ministries, primarily focusing on governance, capacity building, and leadership development.

As an ordained minister, McClinton is an integral member of the leadership team at Maranath Church in Chicago, where Stephen and Candy LaFlora are the pastors.

McClinton resides in Chicago with his wife Tammie and their children.

For more information on speaking invitations, training seminars, or nonprofit consultation services by Rev. McClinton E. Porter, please contact him at the following address:

Rev. McClinton E. Porter

c/o Maranatha Church

6841 S. State Street

Chicago, IL 60637

Email: mcclintonporter@ymail.com

Twitter: @mporter462

Facebook: www.facebook.com/mcclinton.porter

CPSIA information can be obtained
at www.ICGtesting.com
Printed in the USA
BVHW082348080620
581027BV00003B/174